The Rhyme of Birds:

The Wild Birds

By

Andrew Anthony C. Angus

Copyright Page

Copyright © 2017 by Andrew Anthony C. Angus

2nd edition.

All rights reserved.

Ebook ISBN:

ISBN-13: 978-1543256550

Paperback book ISBN:

ISBN-10: 1543256554

.

No part of this book may be reproduced or distributed in any form or by any means or stored in a database or retrieval system, without the prior written permission of the author or publisher/s except as permitted under the Copyright Act of 1976.

Prologue

This is the first poetry book in a series of books about Birdlandia. This poetry book is titled, "The Rhyme of Birds: The Wild Birds".

This poetry book is a "poetic fable". A fable is a story about animals. So, a "poetic fable" is a fable in poem form.

This poetic fable in this book is about an American bald eagle who meets different wild birds (peacock, crane, owl, ostrich) while perched on a juniper tree. The birds dislike each other and the birds try to find a common ground. The juniper tree is located in Birdlandia, a fictional place in California.

Most writers write fables in prose form. Examples are: Rudyard Kipling's "The Jungle Book", George Orwell's "Animal Farm", just to name a few. But, I decided to write a fable in poetry form or what I call "poetic fable".

What inspired me to write this very long poem which I gave the title, "The Rhyme of Birds"?

I always wanted to write a story in poem form. Every aspiring writer either writes their stories in prose or poem. I chose poetry to tell some of my stories.

In 2003, I composed a poem titled, "Peacock Vanity". I submitted it to a poem contest but it did not win.

In 2017 of January, I bought some classic poetry books of William Shakespeare and Samuel Taylor Coleridge in Amazon online bookstore. While reading these classic poems (ex. Shakespeare's poem, "The Phoenix and The Turtle" and Coleridge's poem, "The Rime of the Ancient Mariner"), I felt inspired to write a story about animals in poetry form.

At the same time, in the year 2017 in January, while I was cleaning my room and sorting my paper files, I re-discovered my short poem, "Peacock Vanity" among my old poem files. I remember I wrote this short poem "Peacock Vanity" in 2003. I felt inspired to expand my short poem "Peacock Vanity" into a long poetic fable which is now in this poem book.

I felt so inspired that I finished the first draft of 80 quatrains in just 3 days. Then, I expanded my first draft from 80 quatrains to more than 200 quatrains within the month of February of 2017.

This poetry book uses a quatrain style (i.e. stanza of four lines). Each quatrain is numbered as Q1 for Quatrain 1, Q2 for Quatrain 2 and so on.

Then, the author divides this long poetry by way of a "sonit". I define a "sonit" as a poem with 16 "monologue lines" to differentiate it from a "sonnet" which is a poem that has 14 "non-monologue" lines. Then, a set of 5 sonits comprises a chapter.

This long poem is what I call "conversation poetry" which I define as a poem where characters are conversing in "poetic monologues". Each character converses a "poetic monologue" of four poetic lines. I am trying to popularize this new type of poetry which I call "conversation poetry".

I just coined the term "conversation poetry" to distinguish it from "narrative poetry".

What is the difference between "narrative poetry" and "conversation poetry" ?

In "narrative poetry", the poet simply tells a story using poetry. In "conversation poetry", the poet uses characters to converse in poetic monologues.

This poetry book is a long "conversation poetry" with a total of 100 quatrains divided into 25 sonits and 5 chapters. The four major characters in this poetry book are the four wild birds: Mr. Bald Eagle, Mr. Peacock, Mr. Crane and Mrs. Owl.

In my long poem, each chapter ends with a one-statement moral lesson. Like most fables, one-statement moral lesson or "epigram" are placed at the end of a chapter story.

Aesop, an ancient Greek story teller, ended his fables with a one-statement moral lesson in what is now known as "Aesop's Fables". I could have titled this poem book as "Andrew's Fables" but I decided to title this book as "The Rhyme of Birds".

I placed an "Appendix 1 – Moral Lessons Summary" at the end of this long conversation poetry. The "Appendix 1 – Moral Lessons Summary" is a summary of the one-statement moral lessons of each chapter story.

I also placed an "Appendix 2 – Glossary". This glossary contains words that are used in this poetry book. The glossary is placed to help the readers understand the words and avoid misunderstanding of the words used in the poem. The glossary is helpful for kids, teens, adults and foreigners who are learning the English language.

Finally, I released a second poetry book about Birdlandia which is available also in Amazon.com under the title, "The Rhyme of Birds 2". The second poetry book introduces new characters like Mr. Lyrebird, Mr. Vulture, Mr. Cockatoo, just to name a few.

Author Page

The author's full name is Andrew Anthony C. Angus. Andrew was born in the city of Manila in Luzon, which is an island located in the north of the Philippines.

Andrew started writing poetry during his college days (1992-1996) in Cagayan de Oro City in the province of Misamis Oriental, which in turn, is found in the region called Northern Mindanao. The region is found in Mindanao, which is an island located in the south of the Philippines.

Andrew arrived in California in August 1999 and stayed with his parents living in San Jose, California.

Andrew won his first script writing contest in May 2012 when he won first place for his 2-page very short script entitled, "Lyre for Sale". He got 75 dollars as a cash prize for first place.

In the year 2015, Andrew expanded his 2-page very short script "Lyre for Sale" into a 35-page short script play as a draft entitled, "Pegasus" between April to May 2015.

Also in the year 2015, Andrew finished writing his first comedy screenplay at 125 pages between April to May 2015. The comedy screenplay was tentatively titled, "Pretty Boys/ Pretty Girls". The comedy is about 3 boys from Pennsylvania who were accidentally enrolled in an exclusive college for girls in San Francisco, California.

In the year 2016, Andrew expanded his 35-page short stageplay, "Pegasus" into an 80-page stage play titled, "Hermes and Pegasus". He published his stageplay as book titled, "Hermes and Pegasus: A Stage Play for College and Broadway." in July 2016.

Also in the year 2016, Andrew finished writing his second comedy screenplay which was tentatively titled, "Pretty Boys/Pretty Girls: Revenge of the Dormers". The screenplay was published in book form in August 2016.

Also in the year 2016, Andrew published his poem book, titled, "The Taj Mahal: Quatrains 1 to 80". The poem book is a lyrical poem about the poet's ode to the Taj Mahal.

In the year 2017, Andrew published his second poem book, titled, "The Rhyme of Birds: The Wild Birds". The poem book is a nature poem and a poetic fable about a bald eagle who meets different wild birds in a juniper tree.

Author's Books

I. Screen plays

Andrew published two screenplays in book form:

    a. "Pretty Boys/ Pretty Girls" (Oct 10, 2015). This is a comedy about three boys from Pennsylvania who were accidentally enrolled in an exclusive school for girls in San Francisco, California.

    b. "Pretty Boys/ Pretty Girls: Revenge of the Dormers" (Aug 31, 2016). This is a comedy about three boys from New York who were accidentally enrolled in an exclusive school for girls in San Francisco, California.

II. Stage plays

Andrew published his first stage play in book format last July 5, 2016 via Lulu.com.

    a. "Hermes and Pegasus: A Stageplay for College and Broadway" (Jul 2016). The stageplay is about a king of Troy, King Tros, who wants to have Pegasus for his royal stable.

III. Poetry books

Andrew released two poetry books in the year 2016 and 2017 respectively. One poetry book is a long lyrical poem released in 2016. The second poetry book is a long conversation poem released in 2017.

a. "The Taj Mahal: Quatrains 1 to 80" (November 11, 2016). This poetry book is a lyrical poem about the poet's ode to the Taj Mahal.

b. "The Rhyme of Birds: The Wild Birds" (February 22, 2017). The poetry book is a poetic fable about a bald eagle who meets different wild birds and animals in Birdlandia.

Author's Audio/ Music albums

The author also plays the piano and the guitar.

The author released some of his songs for sale in digital format and CD format starting in 2013 in various online music stores like Itunes, Amazon, Google Play, etc. Links to itunes: https://itunes.apple.com/us/artist/andrew-angus/id204242642

The titles of his music albums are:

a. "Hey Girl Are You Happy" (2013, single)
b. "Just Kiss My Lips" (2013, single)
c. "Tribute for Marilyn" (2013, single)
d. "Fantastic Superhero" (2013, e.p.)
e. "Billionaire" (2014, single)
f. "Let's Rock This World" (2014, single)
g. "Christmas in California" (2014, single)

My songs are available in my Youtube channel:

https://www.youtube.com/user/andrewangusmusic/videos

Table of Contents

Contents	Page
Title Page	i
Copyright Page	ii
Prologue	iii - vi
Author Page	vii - viii
Author's Books	ix - x
Author's Audio/Music Albums	xi
Table of Contents	xii - xiv
Chapter 1: The Bald Eagle	1
Sonit 1: Q1 - Q4	2-3
Sonit 2: Q5 - Q8	4-5
Sonit 3: Q9 - Q12	6-7
Sonit 4: Q13 - Q16	8-9
Sonit 5: Q17 - Q20	10-11
Chapter 2: The Peacock	12
Sonit 6: Q21 - Q24	13-14

Sonit 7: Q25 - Q28	15-16
Sonit 8: Q29 - Q32	17-18
Sonit 9: Q33 - Q36	19-20
Sonit 10: Q37 - Q40	21-22
Chapter 3: The Crane	23
Sonit 11: Q41 - Q44	24-25
Sonit 12: Q45 - Q48	26-27
Sonit 13: Q49 - Q52	28-29
Sonit 14: Q53 - Q56	30-31
Sonit 15: Q57 - Q60	32-33
Chapter 4. The Owl	34
Sonit 16: Q61 - Q64	35-36
Sonit 17: Q65 - Q68	37-38
Sonit 18: Q69 - Q72	39-40
Sonit 19: Q73 - Q76	41-42
Sonit 20: Q77 - Q80	43-44
Chapter 5. The Ostrich	45
Sonit 21: Q81 - Q84	46-47
Sonit 22: Q85 - Q88	48-49

Sonit 23: Q89 - Q92	50-51
Sonit 24: Q93 - Q96	52-53
Sonit 25: Q97 - Q100	54-55
Appendix 1: Moral Lesson Summary	56
Appendix 2: Glossary	57-70
Reader's Notes	71-72

Chapter 1: The Bald Eagle

Chapter 1: The Bald Eagle

Sonit 1

Q1.   Mr. Bald Eagle:

The Bald Eagle lands on juniper tree!

I'm so tired. I need all the sleep I need!

No one disturbs me as I sleep soundly.

I beg the wind not to disturb! Please heed!

Q2.   Mr. Deer:

Wake up! An eagle has landed on tree!

Wake up herd of deer! Let's get out of here!

The eagle might eat our fawns in a spree!

The eagle is so strong and without peer!

Q3.   Mrs. Deer:

Run deer run! I suggest run for your lives!

Run! This is a matter of life and death!

Run to the valley! Run with your deer wives!

Eagle is real! Eagle is not a myth!

Q4.   Mr. Bald Eagle:

Oh yes! A cute fawn! It looks delicious!

But I'm not hungry! I just ate a fish!

The wind must stop howling! I am serious!

I think I should start an eagle's wish dish!

Chapter 1: The Bald Eagle

Sonit 2

Q5.   Mr. Squirrel:

Bald Eagle landed on juniper tree!

Wake up squirrels! Let's get out of this tree!

Let's go to another juniper tree,

Before Bald Eagle eats us in a spree!

Q6.   Mrs. Squirrel:

Mister Bald Eagle! Get out of this tree!

This tree is not for predator eagles!

We live here! This tree is squirrel country!

This tree is for a squadron of squirrels!

Q7.   Mr. Bald Eagle:

Do not disturb me you noisy squirrels!

I am tired! I want to rest on this tree!

This tree is for squirrels and for eagles!

Why don't you want to share this tree with me!

Q8.   Mr. Squirrel:

We don't like an eagle as our neighbor!

You are a predator! We are the prey!

Please just leave! We won't ask any favor!

We must not see you at the end of day!

Chapter 1: The Bald Eagle

Sonit 3:

Q9.   Mr. Bald Eagle:

I will not leave this large juniper tree!

There's enough room for squirrels and eagles!

I will not transfer to another tree!

There's enough room for eagles and seagulls!

Q10.   Mrs. Squirrel:

In that case, we have to leave this huge tree!

This tree is not for predators and preys!

You'll just eat us squirrels as meals for free!

We'll leave this tree like it's the end of days!

Q11.　Mr. Bald Eagle:

I won't ask you any little favor!

It's enough that you leave at once this tree!

Please, gather all the fruits of your labor!

I don't eat juniper berries you see!

Q12.　Mr. Squirrel:

Attention! Soren Squirrel's family!

We have to leave now this juniper tree!

Gather all your valuable property!

Harvest all juniper berries you see!

Chapter 1: The Bald Eagle

Sonit 4

Q13.   Mr. Bald Eagle:

I am not being a bully! Am I?

I know I am strong but am I pushy?

It's either you're too young or old to die!

Death hates the living! Death claims its booty!

Q14.   Mrs. Squirrel:

I am not afraid of death, Bald Eagle!

I want to live life as much as I can!

Squadron of squirrels versus one eagle!

We can beat you! The many versus one!

Q15.   Mr. Bald Eagle:

It's not my fault I was born predator!

A law of nature dictates I eat prey!

That is why I am a strong survivor

Survival of the fittest! Nature's way!

Q16.   Mrs. Squirrel:

I won't apologize for being small!

Small is deadly! Small things can hurt the eye!

Elephants are afraid of mice so small!

Don't harass us if you don't want to die!

Chapter 1: The Bald Eagle

Sonit 5

Q17.   Mr. Bald Eagle:

I am not saying you're a weak creature!

You are so small yet you are pugnacious!

Eating a squirrel is not my leisure!

My leisure's eating fish! That's delicious!

Q18.   Mrs. Squirrel:

Talk is cheap! Let's go! Enough is enough!

Time is acorn! No more conversation!

Let's leave squadron of squirrels! Let's be tough!

There's strength in uniting squirrel nation!

Q19.   Mr. Bald Eagle:

Goodbye squirrels! Please, don't come back again!

I am not in the mood to fight squirrels!

I am tired! I am glad there is no rain!

Please just leave! I don't want any quarrels!

Q20.   Mr. Squirrel:

Bye Bald Eagle! We do not have a choice!

We can't live with a predator neighbor!

All squirrels are leaving! Hope you rejoice!

It's painful to leave this tree we favor!

Chapter 2: The Peacock

Chapter 2: The Peacock

Sonit 6

Q21.   Mr. Peacock:

The peacock's landing on juniper tree!

I'm exhausted! I need my beauty sleep!

Sleep is a right! Sleep is forever free!

I'm glad I'm alive after a long trip!

Q22.   Mr. Bald Eagle:

Where are you from, Mister Peacock with spur?

I see you've landed on juniper tree!

This tree is huge! Plenty of room to spare!

Do you know how to sing with melody?

Q23.   Mr. Peacock:

Oh! You startled me Mister Bald Eagle!

You almost scared me to death with your voice!

Perching on this tree, I hope it's legal!

I thought I was hearing a lion's voice!

Q24.   Mr. Bald Eagle:

I welcome you to this juniper tree!

I'm happy to share this tree with peacocks!

I hope you can sing with a melody!

I do not like the sound of quacking ducks!

Chapter 2: The Peacock

Sonit 7

Q25.   Mr. Peacock:

I have a good voice but not for eagles!

I use my sweet voice for courting peahens!

I have my own share of bird fight struggles!

Look! Squirrels are leaving! They look so tense!

Q26.   Mr. Bald Eagle:

I'm first to perch on this juniper tree!

So, I think this is my territory!

Please leave this tree if you are not friendly!

But, if you're friendly, I can share this tree!

Q27.   Mr. Peacock:

If you don't mind I need my beauty sleep!

We can be good friends Bald Eagle! Why not?

We can be friends after my beauty sleep!

I need rest! I don't want my quills to rot!

Q28.   Mr. Bald Eagle:

Spare me the drama, Mister Peacock bird!

This tree is too big for the two of us!

I want you out of this tree, not a word!

You are so full of yourself! You're a fuss!

Chapter 2: The Peacock

Sonit 8

Q29.   Mr. Peacock:

Stay within your space! I'll stay in my space!

Don't be fussy! There's enough room to spare!

Just respect my space! I'll respect your space!

Stop bullying me or I'll use my spur!

Q30.   Mr. Bald Eagle:

Spur or talon? Who do you think will win?

Your long train makes you easy to defeat!

My talons are sharp! So easy to win!

My talons can turn you into fresh meat!

Q31.   Mr. Peacock:

This bird is not afraid of your wild kind!

You think you can defeat me in this tree?

Don't underestimate me and my kind!

What will you get if you start to eat me?

Q32.   Mr. Bald Eagle:

I won't get anything by eating you!

I don't want any trouble! So just go!

I'm not bullying you! I'm asking you!

You're a fancy bird! You deserve a show!

Chapter 2: The Peacock

Sonit 9

Q33.   Mr. Peacock:

Really? Is that how you treat your bird guest?

Do not underestimate my beauty!

In your opinion, which bird trait is best?

The might of his talons or his beauty?

Q34.   Mr. Bald Eagle:

Beauty can be a liability!

Worrying how you look is waste of time!

My talons speak my credibility!

You're fancy! You have no reason nor rhyme!

Q35.   Mr. Squirrel:

Excuse me! I forgot my nutcracker!

Don't mind me! Just continue your debate!

I promise I will leave this juniper!

Just bear with me! I will not be so late!

Q36.   Mr. Bald Eagle:

A peacock's beauty can cause his downfall!

I am a fighter! That is my nature!

And an eagle does not eat an eagle!

That does not help in building one's stature!

Chapter 2: The Peacock

Sonit 10

Q37.   Mr. Peacock:

The eagle's pride can lead to his downfall!

Might is right! But might can also be wrong!

Truth is powerful! Truth is beautiful!

I must spread my beauty while I am young!

Q38.   Mr. Bald Eagle:

The bonfire of vanities is burning!

I hope you don't burn with your vanity!

I don't want to see you in the evening!

Bring your fancy plumage out of this tree!

Q39.   Mr. Peacock:

Yes, I am fancy! Yes, I am beauty!

My fancy plumage attracts the ladies!

I need to replicate my kind beauty!

I'm no fighter! I'm a lover of peace!

Q40.   Mr. Bald Eagle:

Mister Peacock, you are the vainest bird!

You will lose your beauty when you retire!

You're the vanity of vanities, bird!

You want to be thrown into the bonfire?

Chapter 3: The Crane

Chapter 3: The Crane

Sonit 11

Q41.   Mr. Crane:

Hello everyone! I am Mister Crane!

I'm looking for a tree to roost and rest!

I see Mister Peacock's beautiful train!

I see the Bald Eagle sits on the west!

Q42.   Mr. Peacock:

I won't lose my beauty when I retire!

My beauty is sung by chirping crickets.

My beauty is praised with a poet's lyre!

Beauty, so immortalized by poets!

Q43.   Mr. Crane:

Mister Bald Eagle, you're just plain envy!

Mister Peacock is famous in Asia!

Peacock's fanlike plumage is found only

In Congo, Persia, Burma and India!

Q44.   Mr. Peacock:

Thank you Mister Crane for your flattery.

My ego is boosted at an instance!

I once saw cranes painted on pottery.

I know you're an expert in courtship dance!

Chapter 3: The Crane

Sonit 12

Q45.   Mr. Crane:

The peacock's beauty is legendary!

But I prefer function over beauty!

Beautiful birds can be sedentary.

Displaying their beauty is their duty!

Q46.   Mr. Bald Eagle:

I'd rather be strong than be beautiful.

I'd rather be predator than a prey!

I'd rather fly in the sky like a gull

Than to stay and walk on the ground all day!

Q47.   Mr. Peacock:

To be strongest or to be prettiest?

I'd rather be prettiest of all birds!

Note! A beautiful bird is not a pest!

Peacocks are inspiration to most bards!

Q48.   Mr. Crane:

I may not be the strongest wing flyer,

But I prefer to stay and nest on ground.

I must always be aware for danger,

As I live on ground where humans are found!

Chapter 3: The Crane

Sonit 13

Q49.   Mr. Bald Eagle:

A bird cannot live long by being cute!

A bird needs strength to lead his family!

Might is the best trait. I will not refute!

To be cute in the wild is plain silly!

Q50.   Mr. Crane:

I agree. A bird needs strength to survive!

Nature is no respecter of wild birds!

Strong beasts eat the weak beasts to be alive!

Nature's laws are hidden, unwritten words!

Q51.   Mr. Peacock:

I'm not a cute bird! Cute is for small birds!

I'm a big bird! Handsome is the right word!

Peacocks are handsome birds and not cute birds!

I have a spur which I use like a sword!

Q52.   Mr. Crane:

Beautiful birds are pleasant to the eyes!

Cranes are not that beautiful for display!

I prefer to dance than to catch a mice!

Long legs are essential to dance in bay!

Chapter 3: The Crane

Sonit 14

Q53.   Mr. Bald Eagle:

I do not have long legs but that is fine!

I prefer to soar the sky than to dance!

My talons help me to fish and to dine.

My talons function well like a sharp lance!

Q54.   Mr. Crane:

I'm a dancer and a martial artist!

Cranes treat dance as the highest form of art!

Without dance, we cranes will never exist!

I can teach basic dance steps for a start!

Q55.   Mr. Peacock:

You seem to be a nice guy Mister Crane!

But dancing is not my thingamajig!

My hobby is fanning my feather train!

Peahens go crazy when my fan is big!

Q56.   Mr. Crane:

Fanning out your feather train is lovely!

I wish I have a plumage with a shine!

Your feathers glisten! It is so catchy!

But I am grateful! My plumage is fine!

Chapter 3: The Crane

Sonit 15

Q57.   Mr. Squirrel:

Excuse me wild birds! I found my gizmo!

I found my nutcracker up high this tree!

Continue your debate. I have to go!

Goodbye strangers! I will miss this old tree!

Q58.   Mr. Bald Eagle:

Hey look! Two bird hunters in Birdlandia!

Those humans are very dangerous beasts!

We have to drive them out of Birdlandia!

The strangers hold their rifles with their fists!

Q59.   Mr. Peacock:

I hope the bird hunters do not see us!

I hope they go to a different way!

I hope the clouds turn into a nimbus!

So that rain will fall and drive them away!

Q60.   Mr. Crane:

I hope the strangers hunt non-bird species!

Like a deer or a boar or a panther!

It hurts me when birds are cut to pieces!

Look! The humans are moving out farther!

Chapter 4: The Owl

Chapter 4: The Owl

Sonit 16

Q61.   Mr. Bald Eagle:

Look! A bird is coming towards this tree!

It has huge eyes! I think it is an owl!

Is this flying bird, a he or a she?

Most birds know that an owl is a night fowl!

Q62.   Mr. Peacock:

I think a she-owl is coming to town!

Female owls are bigger than the male owls!

Birdland is a place for birds so renown!

What's more famous than the hooting of owls?

Q63.   Mrs. Owl:

Hoot! Hello to all the birds on this tree!

I can see three males against one female!

I am outnumbered but I am not wee!

I'm wise enough to mingle with a tale!

Q64.   Mr. Crane:

What tale of owl do you bring for us three?

A tale of joy or a tale of sadness?

What tale of hoot do you bring to this tree?

I hope it is not a tale of madness!

Chapter 4: The Owl

Sonit 17

Q65.   Mrs. Owl:

I bring an owl's tale of gladness and joy!

Birdlandia is looking for a leader!

The leader must be smart or strong, not coy!

Someone who's serious and not a kidder!

Q66.   Mr. Bald Eagle:

Perhaps, Birdlandia is looking for me!

I think the Birdland needs my leadership!

I am strong, serious and not a bully!

I'm not coy! I'm born for governorship!

Q67.   Mrs. Owl:

Are you smart enough to lead the Birdland?

Bald Eagle is so strong and so mighty!

Who wants to challenge the eagle's strong hand!

Someone who has courage and not flighty!

Q68.   Mr. Peacock:

I think Bald Eagle is such a bully!

He just insulted me for my beauty!

He loves to eat fresh fish like a sushi!

But eagle lacks brains and is not witty!

Chapter 4: The Owl

Sonit 18

Q69.   Mrs. Owl:

Bald Eagle! Bulliest bird of all birds!

You're the strongest bird of all the raptors!

I'm Misis Owl! I'm smartest of all nerds.

I'd rather fly than swim like the gators!

Q70.   Mr. Bald Eagle:

Misis Owl! You're the geekiest of nerds.

But, I prefer to be strong than bird smart!

You're the nerdiest of all the nerd birds!

And my talons can tear flesh as an art!

Q71.   Mr. Crane:

Bald Eagle, king of raptors in the sky!

Misis Owl is queen of nocturnal birds!

I'm king of the dance birds until I die!

Peacock is the queen of colorful birds!

Q72.   Mr. Peacock:

How dare call me queen of colorful birds!

I feel insulted when you call me queen!

I'm king and not queen of colorful birds!

I am so masculine inspite my sheen!

Chapter 4: The Owl

Sonit 19

Q73.   Mrs. Owl:

I prefer to be called queen of smartest!

But, I'll take it: queen of nocturnal birds!

Many poets think owls are the wisest.

At least, I don't prey on the cattle herds!

Q74.   Mr. Bald Eagle:

Yes! I am strong and I love the blue sky!

I won't apologize for being strong!

I am king of raptors until I die!

Might is right! And might is not always wrong!

Q75.   Mr. Peacock:

I won't apologize for my beauty!

I was born this way and I am grateful!

I am beauty but I am not haughty!

I am not ugly and I am thankful!

Q76.   Mr. Crane:

Arnis, taekwondo, karate, kung fu!

I am not afraid of heights or in fights!

My martial art skills will defeat my foe!

Cranes in migrating season love air flights!

Chapter 4: The Owl

Sonit 20

Q77.   Mrs. Owl:

I won't apologize for being smart.

I will not back out of avian debates!

Debate is a skill and my choice of art.

I will kick you out of the forest gates!

Q78.   Mr. Crane:

I will not apologize for my height.

My long legs are useful in martial arts!

I'm on a snail diet for flight or fight.

My legs are so useful in dancing arts!

Q79.   Mrs. Owl:

My eyes are wide especially at night.

I can hear a small mouse at long distance.

I can turn around my head, day or night!

But I cannot sing and I cannot dance!

Q80.   Mr. Peacock:

I do not know how to dance while courting.

My lovely plumage train attracts females!

My ocelli lure peahens for mating!

My colorful plumage train never fails!

Chapter 5: The Ostrich

Chapter 5: The Ostrich

Sonit 21

Q81.   Mr. Peacock:

Look over there! An ostrich is running!

Are there ostriches in California?

He or she is escaping from something!

What's an ostrich doing in Birdlandia?

Q82.   Mrs. Owl:

Here it comes! The ostrich is approaching!

Ostriches are not native to Persia!

It looks like the ostrich is panicking!

I know ostriches live in Africa!

Q83.   Ms. Ostrich:

Help! Help! I don't want to be cooked as lunch!

An ostrich rancher is looking for me!

I don't want to go back to Ostrich Ranch!

Eagle! Please hide me! Peacock! Please hide me!

Q84.   Mr. Bald Eagle:

I want to help you but you're too heavy!

You want me to bring you up on this tree?

You must climb a ladder or a levee!

Then, you can perch on a branch of this tree!

Chapter 5: The Ostrich

Sonit 22

Q85.   Mr. Crane:

Just hide behind this tree of juniper!
You will not be seen behind this tall tree!
Hide! If you want to escape the rancher!
If the rancher passes by, then you're free!

Q86.   Mrs. Owl:

If the rancher misses you, then you're good!
Where did the ostrich rancher get you, girl?
Is the rancher raising you as meat food?
You must be prized like an expensive pearl!

Q87.   Mr. Peacock:

Ostrich meat is tasty and exotic!

I heard ostrich eggs are so flavorful!

Not to put you in a state of panic,

Ostrich meat is known to be savorful!

Q88.   Ms. Ostrich:

Oh well! I'll hide behind this juniper!

I hope the rancher does not see me here!

I hope the rancher will just disappear!

To be fried ostrich is my greatest fear!

Chapter 5: The Ostrich

Sonit 23

Q89.   Mr. Bald Eagle:

Miss Ostrich, you are so tall and bulky!

You're just in time in our live discussion!

You have long legs, your body is hulky!

Hope you don't trip and get a concussion!

Q90.   Ms. Ostrich:

What discussion are you talking about?

Does it concern me or other tall birds?

I am so tall! I'm glad I have no gout!

Do you know my rancher owns ostrich herds?

Q91.   Mr. Crane:

We were discussing what bird trait is best!

I told these birds, tall height is the best trait!

I use my long legs in my wading quest!

I want to hear from you! I cannot wait!

Q92.   Ms. Ostrich:

My best trait is definitely long legs!

My height is a superior advantage!

My legs are like walking sticks or long pegs!

But sometimes, height is a disadvantage!

Chapter 5: The Ostrich

Sonit 24

Q93.　Mrs. Owl:

We'll just call you: queen of long legged birds!

Every bird here has a royal title!

You're the tallest among long legged birds!

You run so fast, not like a slow turtle!

Q94.　Ms. Ostrich:

Miss Olongleg Ostrich is my full name!

I'm from Somalia but I live here now!

Queen of long legged birds! I like it dame!

Thank you for the royal title somehow!

Q95.   Mr. Peacock:

Miss Ostrich, your long legs are an asset!

Your legs can run fast and tear any flesh!

Can you outrun a cheetah or a jet?

At least, you'll enjoy here, the air so fresh!

Q96.   Ms. Ostrich:

I want to be a free bird like you four!

How I wish I can fly up this tall tree!

Living in an ostrich ranch is a bore!

If only I can fly, I will be free!

Chapter 5: The Ostrich

Sonit 25

Q97.　Mr. Ostrich Rancher:

Dang! There you are Miss Ostrich Escaper!

I can see you hiding behind the tree!

You're running away like an eloper!

Come back to your ostrich ranch family!

Q98.　Ms. Ostrich:

Goodbye flock of birds on the tall tree branch!

I have to outrun my captor again!

I don't want to go back to ostrich ranch!

I think it's time for me to run a lane!

Q99.   Mr. Bald Eagle:

Poor Miss Ostrich. We can't do anything!

If I attack the rancher, I'll be killed!

The rancher's rifle is set for shooting!

If the rancher drives so fast, I'll get wheeled!

Q100.   Mr. Crane:

Anyway! Let's go back to discussion!

We were discussing about bird's best traits!

Let's start a new round of conversation!

I think Miss Ostrich is now in dire straits!

Appendix 1: Moral Lesson Summary

I compiled all the moral lessons of each chapter into one appendix. What are the moral lessons of each chapter?

Chapter 1: The Eagle.
Moral Lesson: A prey cannot trust its predator.

Chapter 2: The Peacock.
Moral Lesson. Beauty is an advantage but it can also be a liability.

Chapter 3: The Crane.
Moral Lesson: Strangers are either potential new friends or new enemies.

Chapter 4: The Owl.
Moral Lesson: Flattery is sometimes necessary in making friendships.

Chapter 5: The Ostrich
Moral Lesson: Height is a superior advantage and also a disadvantage.

Appendix 2: Glossary

To avoid confusion in reading my long poem, I provided a glossary. The following are words used in the poem. The meanings are given as used in the poem. This glossary is useful for kids, teens, adults and foreigners who are learning the English language. There are 85 words in the glossary.

-A-

Acorn. Noun. 1. A nut of the oak tree. (Ex. Squirrels love to eat acorns.) (The word is used in Chapter 1: The Bald Eagle.)

Advantage. Noun. 1. A benefit. 2. Any thing or circumstance that favors someone to success or achievement. (Ex. He used his wealth to his advantage.) (The word is used in Chapter 5: The Ostrich.)

Apologize. Verb. 1. To offer an expression of regret or sorry for some fault or injury. (Ex. The students apologize to their teacher. (The word is used in Chapter 1: The Bald Eagle.)

Arnis. Noun. 1. a Filipino martial arts using sticks, instead of swords, in fighting. (Ex. He is skillful in arnis aside from fencing.) (The word is used in Chapter 4: The Owl.)

Art. Noun. 1. An object or action that is considered beautiful. (Ex. Hip hop is now considered an art.) (The word is used in Chapter 3: The Crane.)

Asset. Noun. 1. A desirable thing or quality. (Ex. Her face is her asset.) (The word is used in Chapter 5: The Ostrich.)

Avian. Adjective. 1. related to birds. (Ex. Many avian issues are discussed by bird scientists.) (The word is used in Chapter 4: The Owl.)

-B-

Bald Eagle. Noun. 1. A large fish-eating eagle, found in Canada and United States, having a dark golden-brown back and wings while the head and tail is covered with white feathers in the adult. (Ex. The bald eagle caught a fish with its talons.) (The word is used in Chapter 1: The Bald Eagle.)

Bard. Noun. 1. A poet who delivers vocally a poem. (Ex. The bard read his latest poem.) (The word is used in Chapter 3: The Crane.)

Berry. Noun. 1. Any small fleshy fruit with seeds. (Ex. The juniper berry is ripe.) (The word is used in Chapter 1: The Bald Eagle.)

Birdland. Noun. 1. Another word for Birdlandia. (Ex. Let's go the Birdland and see the birds.) (The word is used in Chapter 4: The Owl.) (See Birdlandia.)

Birdlandia. Noun. 1. A fictional place where birds and animals can talk in Andrew's poem fable. (Ex. Birdlandia needs a bird governor.) (The word is used in Chapter 3: The Crane.) (See Birdland.)

Bonfire. Noun. 1. A fire burning in an area in open air. (Ex. We started a bonfire when the sun started to set.) (The word is used in Chapter 2: The Peacock.)

Booty. Noun. 1. spoils of war. 2. any prize. 3. plunder. (Ex. The pirate shared his booty to his crew.) (The word is used in Chapter 1: The Bald Eagle.)

Bully. Noun. 1. a person who harasses or beats up those weaker than him/her. (Ex. Bill was punished because he was a bully.) (The word is used in Chapter 1: The Bald Eagle.)

-C-

Courting. Noun. 1. The act of wooing or seeking affection. (Ex. The man brought roses while courting a female office mate.) (The word is used in Chapter 2: The Peacock.)

Crane. Noun. 1. a marsh bird known for its long legs and its mating dance ritual. (Ex. The crane is wading near the riverbank.) (The word is used in Chapter 3: The Crane.)

Credibility. Noun. 1. Believability. 2. Trustworthiness. (Ex. His credibility is boosted by his high grades.) (The word is used in Chapter 2: The Peacock.)

-D-

Deer. Noun. 1. A hoofed, cud-chewing mammal, the male of which bears antlers. (Ex. The deer loves to eat grass.) (The word is used in Chapter 1: The Bald Eagle.)

Dire. Adjective. 1. dreadful. 2. terrible. (Ex. The ostrich is in dire situation.) (The word is used in Chapter 5: The Ostrich.)

-E-

Eagle. Noun. 1. A large bird of prey known for its talons and curved beak. (Ex. The eagle loves to soar the sky.) (The word is used in Chapter 1: The Bald Eagle.) (See bald eagle.)

-F-

Fancy. Adjective. 1. flamboyant. (Ex. He is a fancy pianist.) 2. overdecorative. (Ex. The table setting is fancy.) 3. showy. (Ex. The bartender is very fancy in preparing a cocktail.) (The word is used in Chapter 2: The Peacock.)

Favor. Noun. 1. Request with a promise or something in return. (Ex. I am asking you a favor.) Verb. 1. To approve. (Ex. The tree is highly favored by the cutter.)(The word is used in Chapter 1: The Bald Eagle.)

Flattery. Noun. 1. excessive praise. (Ex. He likes the flattery coming from his friends.) 2. insincere praise. (Ex. She hates the flattery of her enemies.) (The word is used in Chapter 2: The Peacock.)

Fuss. Noun. 1. someone who is picky or peevish, (Ex. My son is a fuss when eating vegetables.) 2. someone who is a source of unnecessary excitement, (Ex. You do not belong in this group because you are a fuss.) 3. someone who is fancy, (Ex. I like your fancy clothes, you're such a fuss!) 4. someone who is hard to please. (Ex. My boss is such a fuss.) 5. unnecessary excitement. (Ex. What is the fuss all about?) (This word is used in Chapter 2: The Peacock.)

Fussy. Adjective. 1. choosy. 2. hard to please. (Ex. My child is a fussy eater.) 3. grouchy. 4. easily irritated. (Ex. The waiter was so fussy when we asked for water.) 4. causing excitement. (This word is used in Chapter 2: The Peacock.)

-G-

Gator. Noun. 1. An alligator. (Ex. The gator went back to the river.) (The word is used in Chapter 4: The Owl.)

Geeky. Adjective. (geekier, geekiest) 1. Nerdy. 2. Tending to be absorbed in intellectual activities. (Ex. My son is kind of geeky.) (The word is used in Chapter 4: The Owl.)

Gizmo. Noun. 1. A gadget. (Ex. I found a gizmo for cracking nuts.) (The word is used in Chapter 3: The Crane.)

-H-

Heed. Verb. To pay attention. (Ex. Heed the instructions before using the machine.) (The word is used in Chapter 1: The Bald Eagle.)

-I-

Immortalize. Verb. 1. To make famous for eternity. (Ex. The poem immortalized the beauty of the swan.) (The word is used in Chapter 3: The Crane.)

-J-

Juniper. Noun. 1. A name of specific tree that belongs to the genus *Juniperus* which is any evergreen, coniferous shrub or tree and bears blue or black berries. (Ex. The juniper tree was knocked down by the storm.) (The word is first used in Chapter 1: The Bald Eagle)

-K-

Karate. Noun. 1. A Japanese martial arts using only hands, arms, legs, feet in fighting. (Ex. He practiced karate everyday.) (The word is used in Chapter 4: The Owl.)

King. Noun. 1. A male sovereign ruler; the chief authority of a country; a male who reigns a life tenure by hereditary right. (Ex. The king sat on his throne while receiving a guest.) 2. A male person or thing that is considered best in his particular group or profession. (Ex. Chaplin was considered the king of comedy in his time.) (The word is used in Chapter 3: The Crane.)

Kidder. Noun. 1. One who kids or jokes. (Ex. My son is a kidder.) (The word is used in Chapter 4: The Owl.)

Kung Fu. Noun. 1. A Chinese martial arts. (Ex. He was trained in kung fu when he was a teenager.) (The word is used in Chapter 4: The Owl.)

-L-

Leisure. Noun. 1. The activity done during spare time or during rest and recreation. (Ex. My leisure is drawing.) (The word is used in Chapter 1: The Bald Eagle.)

Levee. Noun. 1. An embankment to prevent a river from flooding. (Ex. The levee was destroyed by the flood.)(The word is used in Chapter 5: The Ostrich.)

Liability. Noun. 1. A disadvantage. (Ex. His height is his liability.) (The word is used in Chapter 2: The Peacock.)

-M-

Melody. Noun. 1. a tune. 2. pleasing sounds in sequence. (Ex. He sang a song with a sweet melody.) (The word is used in Chapter 2: The Peacock.)

Myth. Noun. 1. a story (Ex. We are studying Greek myth.) 2. fiction. (ex. His claim of being a war hero is pure myth.) (The word is used in Chapter 1: The Bald Eagle.)

-N-

Nerd. Noun. 1. A person who is too much involved in intellectual activities. 2. A person who is socially awkward. (Ex. Anne doesn't want to be a nerd so she plays volleyball.) (The word is used in Chapter 4: The Owl.)

Nocturnal. Adjective. 1. active at night. (Ex. He is nocturnal.) 2. sleeping at day time but awake at night time. (Ex. The owl is a nocturnal bird.) (The word is used is Chapter 4: The Owl.)

Nutcracker. Noun. 1. An object used for cracking nuts. (Ex. The nutcracker was used to crack the hard walnut.)(The word is used in Chapter 2: The Peacock and Chapter 3: The Crane.)

-O-

Ocelli. Noun. 1. plural form of ocellus. (See ocellus.) (Ex. The peacock's ocelli attracted the crowd.) (The word is used in Chapter 4: The Owl.)

Ocellus. Noun. 1. the eyespot design found in a peacock's train. 2. The singular form of ocelli. (See ocelli.)

Ostrich. Noun. 1. A tall, large, two-toed, flightless bird that is found in Africa and Arabia, having a scientific name: *Struthio Camelus.* (Ex. The female ostrich laid two eggs.) (The word is used in Chapter 5: The Ostrich.)

Owl. Noun. 1. a night bird of prey that usually has a huge circular face, huge eyes and a small hooked beak. (Ex. The owl captured a mouse.) (The word is used in Chapter 4: The Owl.)

-P-

Panther. Noun. 1. a cougar. (Ex. A panther was seen in the rainforest.) (The word is used in Chapter 3: The Crane)

Peacock. Noun. 1. A male peafowl. 2. A male counterpart of a peahen. (Ex. The peacock was transferred to an aviary.) (The word is used in Chapter 2: The Peacock.) (See peafowl and peahen.)

Peafowl. Noun. 1. A bird where the male is known for its beautiful long plumage which can be spread out like a fan. (Ex. A peafowl was placed in a zoo yesterday.) (See peacock and peahen.)

Peahen. Noun. 1. A female peafowl. 2. A female counterpart of a peacock. (See peafowl.) (Ex. The peahen laid three eggs.) (The word is used in Chapter 2: The Peacock.) (See peacock and peafowl.)

Peer. Noun. 1. an equal. (Ex. His talent is without peer.) (The word is used in Chapter 1: The Bald Eagle.)

Perch. Verb. 1. to roost. 2. to alight on an elevated position in order to rest. (Ex. The hawk perched on the fence.)(The word is used in Chapter 2: The Peacock.)

Plumage. Noun. 1. a set of feathers. (Ex. The parrot's plumage is colorful.) (The word is used in Chapter 2: The Peacock.)

Predator. Noun. 1. an animal that hunts weaker animals for its food. (Ex. An eagle is a predator that eats fish.) (The word is used in Chapter 1: The Bald Eagle.)

Pretty. Adjective. 1. quite beautiful. (Ex. She is pretty.) 2. quite (Ex. She is pretty charming.) (The word is used as an adjective and as a noun in Chapter 2: The Peacock.)

Prey. Noun. 1. An animal that is hunted by a stronger animal as food. (Ex. A lion cub is an easy prey to adult hyenas.) (The word is used in Chapter 1: The Bald Eagle.)

Pugnacious. Adjective. 1. combative. 2. feisty. 3. tending to engage in boxing or fist fight. (Ex. Roosters are very pugnacious during cockfighting. (The word is used in Chapter 1: The Bald Eagle.)

-Q-

Quarrel. Noun. 1. An angry dispute. (Ex. Her quarrel with her boss led to her firing.) (The word is used in Chapter 1: The Bald Eagle.)

Queen. Noun. 1. A female ruler who reigns a life tenure by hereditary right. (Ex. The queen prepares her army for battle.) 2. A woman who is considered foremost in her particular group or profession. (Ex. Lucille was queen of comedy in her time.) (The word is used in Chapter 3: The Crane.)

Quest. Noun. 1. An expedition to obtain something. 2. A search to obtain something. (Ex. His quest for clues about the murder has finally ended.) (The word is used in Chapter 5: The Ostrich.)

Quill. Noun. 1. a large feather. (Ex. I used a quill as a pen.) (The word is used in Chapter 2: The Peacock.)

-R-

Raptor. Noun. 1. a bird of prey. (The suspected raptor turned out to be an osprey. (The word is used in Chapter 4: The Owl.)

Roost. Verb. 1. To rest. 2. To perch. (Ex. The falcon is looking for a tree to roost.) (The word is used in Chapter 3: The Crane.)

-S-

Sedentary. Adjective. 1. characterized by much sitting. 2. stationary. (Ex. His job as a cashier is a sedentary task.) (The word is used in Chapter 3: The Crane.)

Sheen. Noun. 1. a luster. 2. a shiny reflection. (Ex. You have a sheen on your cheek.) (The word is used in Chapter 4: The Owl.)

Spree. Noun. 1. A whimsical act or pre-meditated act done in a short period of time. (Ex. She went on a shopping spree on her birthday.) (The word is used in Chapter 1: The Bald Eagle.)

Spur. Noun. 1. a sharp, pointed appendage found on the legs of some birds. (Ex. Roosters use their spurs in fighting.) (The word is used in Chapter 2: The Peacock.)

Squirrel. Noun. 1. A rodent that lives on trees and has a bushy tail. (Ex. A squirrel loves to eat nuts.) (The word is used in Chapter 1: The Bald Eagle.)

Squadron. Noun. 1. a military unit for warships, cavalry, aviation. (Ex. The squadron of fighter planes landed safely.) (The word is used in Chapter 1: The Bald Eagle.)

Staple. Noun. 1. Something necessary to sustain life. (Ex. Bread is staple to Americans.). Adjective. 1. essential to sustain life. (Ex. Milk is a staple food for babies.) (The word is used in Chapter 1: The Bald Eagle.)

Stature. Noun. 1. physical height. 2. status. (Ex. His stature is an advantage in basketball.) (The word is used in Chapter 2: The Peacock.)

Straits. Noun. 1. distress 2. difficulties 3. situation of distress. (Ex. The peacock is in dire straits after being captured.) (The word is used in Chapter 5: The Ostrich.)

Sushi. Noun. 1. A Japanese dish made of rice wrapped in seaweed roll and cut into bite size then topped with raw fish. (Ex. We ordered sushi for lunch.) (The word is used in Chapter 4: The Owl.)

-T-

Taekwondo. Noun. 1. a Korean martial art. (Ex. My cousin studied taekwondo in high school.) (The word is used in Chapter 4: The Owl.)

Talon. Noun. 1. a claw of a bird of prey. (Ex. Eagles used their talons in catching fish.) (The word is used in Chapter 2: The Peacock.)

Territory. Noun. 1. an area protected from intruders. (Ex. The lion defended its territory from the hyenas.) (The word is used in Chapter 2: The Peacock.)

Thingamajig. Noun. 1. Slang for a gadget you don't know the name. 2. Slang word for skill, expertise or specialty. (Ex. Dancing is not my thingamajig.) (The word is used in Chapter 3: The Crane.)

Train. Noun. 1. a special term for the peacock's fanlike plumage. The fanlike plumage is erroneously called "tail" by non-scientists. (Ex. The peacock's train is long and beautiful.) (The word is used in Chapter 2: The Peacock.)

-U-

Underestimate. Verb. 1. To underrate. (Ex. The man underestimated the teen because of his age.) (The word is used in Chapter 2: The Peacock.)

-V-

Vain. Adjective. (Vainer, Vainest) 1. conceited. 2. having excessive regard of oneself. 3. having no real value. 4. futile. (Ex. He is a vain politician who always grabs the limelight.) Idiom. In vain. 1. Without purpose. (Ex. He did not die in vain as his heroic deed is now recorded in history.) (The word is used in Chapter 2: The Peacock.)

Vanity. Noun. 1. The state of being vain. 2. conceitedness. 3. state of having no real value. (Ex. He was not accepted to the science club because of his vanity.) (The word is used in Chapter 2: The Peacock.)

-W-

Wee. Adjective. 1. Small. (Ex. He was not accepted in football because he is wee.) (The word is used in Chapter 4: The Owl.)

-X-

-Y-

Young. Adjective. 1. Not old. (Ex. She was so young when she started college.) (The word is used in Chapter 1: The Bald Eagle.)

-Z-

Reader's Notes

Reader's Notes

Made in the USA
Las Vegas, NV
16 December 2021